GRUDGE: UNDERSTANDING RESENTMENT, JUSTICE, AND THE DESIRE TO BE HEARD

First edition. July 14, 2025.

ISBN: 979-8231628827

Written by Dr. Hussam Atef Elkhatib.

Table of Contents

Grudge: Understanding Resentment, Justice, and the Desire to Be Heard

Disclaimer

This book is a work of nonfiction informed by psychological theory, ethical inquiry, and real-world observation. While it draws on academic research and lived experiences, it is not intended to serve as a substitute for professional medical, psychological, legal, or therapeutic advice.

The content within reflects the author's interpretations, analyses, and reflections, and is meant to invite critical thought and emotional exploration. Readers are encouraged to approach the themes within this book with both openness and discernment, especially if they are working through personal trauma or complex emotional histories.

The aim of this work is not to justify hostility or promote long-term resentment, but rather to understand the human experience of being hurt, unheard, and morally unsettled—and to explore what it means to seek acknowledgment, accountability, and peace.

Dedication

For those who have carried pain in silence—
Not out of vengeance,
But because no one ever truly listened.
And for those who continue to seek justice,
Not to punish,
But to be seen.

Special Dedication

To my beautiful wife, Kazumichan, for her utmost support throughout all my ups and downs.

Preface: Why This Book Matters Now

There are emotions we readily admit to—sadness, anger, joy, even fear. But resentment? The word itself feels taboo, almost shameful, as though acknowledging it makes us bitter or morally flawed. Society has long promoted the virtues of forgiveness, equating it with strength, healing, and higher morality. And while forgiveness can indeed be transformative, the near-universal demand to "let go" of resentment often comes without nuance, without compassion, and—most dangerously—without listening.

This book was born from a question that lingered in my mind for years: *Why do we hold grudges?* What makes certain emotional wounds so enduring that, even after apologies are offered or time has passed, the pain persists? Are we merely being stubborn—or is there something meaningful and even morally valid in holding on?

In my own life and through conversations with others—students, friends, patients, colleagues—I have seen how deeply the experience of being wronged can shape our identity. I have seen people wrestle with whether they should forgive someone who never apologized. I have seen how a grudge can feel like the only proof that a violation happened at all. And I have learned that, often, people don't want revenge or retaliation—they want to be heard, validated, and respected. They want their pain to matter.

Grudge: Understanding Resentment, Justice, and the Desire to Be Heard is not a guidebook on how to forgive. It is not a moral indictment of those who cannot let go. Rather, it is an exploration of the emotional logic behind holding a grudge—an attempt to understand what it means, what it protects, what it signals, and what it asks of us.

We live in a time of global reckoning with pain—personal, historical, and collective. We are reexamining stories we were once told to accept, naming harms that were once silenced, and refusing to move on until we are truly seen. In this context, the grudge is not merely a petty feeling—it can be a form of resistance, a signal of injustice, or a call for restoration.

Throughout this book, I draw upon psychology, philosophy, personal narrative, cultural studies, and spiritual traditions. I aim to approach the grudge not as a weakness to be eliminated but as a symptom to be interpreted, a message worth decoding. Sometimes, holding on is the only way we know how to survive. Other times, it is the voice of our dignity refusing to be ignored.

My hope is that this book will validate what many have felt but could not articulate. That it will open conversations we've long avoided. And that it will allow you, the reader, to navigate the complexities of your emotional life with greater clarity, compassion, and freedom.

You are not alone in what you carry. Let's begin.

Introduction: The Unspoken Weight of a Grudge

There is a silence that lives beneath the surface of many of our conversations—a silence shaped by something we don't often name aloud: the grudge. Not the cartoonish, bitter caricature we associate with lifelong feuds or spiteful revenge, but the quiet, persistent feeling that something remains unresolved. A wound, a betrayal, an injustice—unhealed and unacknowledged.

Grudges carry a reputation. They are labeled as petty, immature, or even poisonous. We are taught from a young age that to forgive is noble and to forget is divine. We are told to "move on," to "let it go," to "be the bigger person." And when we can't—when the ache remains or the memory resurfaces—we begin to feel ashamed of our inability to release the pain. As though holding on to hurt is itself a character flaw.

But what if it's not?

What if the grudge is not merely a flaw in our emotional system, but a message? A sign that something still matters, that justice was not done, that closure was never truly reached? What if resentment is the voice of our unmet needs—our need for acknowledgment, respect, fairness, or safety—speaking through the cracks of our silence?

In my years of exploring human behavior, I've come to believe that the grudge is not a sickness of the soul, but a symptom of moral memory. It is not about an inability to forgive, but an inability to forget what was never addressed. It is the quiet protest of the wounded, the unheard, the wronged—and it is far more common than we admit.

This book is not an invitation to nurse grievances or glorify bitterness. It is, instead, a space to examine the deeper layers of what we call a "grudge"—to ask why it arises, how it shapes us, what it seeks, and whether it can be transformed without being erased. It is an exploration of that liminal space between hurt and healing, where justice and empathy meet, and where moral truth is often clearer than emotional resolution.

You will not find in these pages a prescription for how to forgive, nor a simple list of steps to move on. Instead, you will find an honest inquiry into the psychological, relational, and cultural forces that shape the way we hold on—and sometimes, the way we must.

We will look at the science of emotional memory. We will unpack the stories we tell about forgiveness. We will consider how grudges manifest in our relationships, our identities, and our faith traditions. And most importantly, we will listen to the voice beneath the grudge—the one that has waited too long to be heard.

If you have ever carried pain that others dismissed...

If you have struggled to forgive and wondered what that says about you...

If you have found yourself asking why a wound still stings, even after all this time...

This book is for you.

Let us begin—not with the demand to let go, but with the courage to look within.

Chapter 1: What Is a Grudge, Really?

Most of us think we know what a grudge is. It's something we accuse others of holding—never ourselves. It's a word laced with judgment, often used to discredit someone's pain or moral position: "They're still holding a grudge," we say, as if to dismiss both the person and their story. But what is a grudge, really? Where does it come from, and why does it linger?

To begin this exploration honestly, we must first strip the grudge of its stigma. A grudge is not always born of bitterness or vengeance. At its core, a grudge is a response to unresolved harm. It is the internal echo of an experience that has not been fully acknowledged, validated, or healed. It is memory fused with emotion—specifically, moral emotion. And unlike fleeting irritation, a grudge endures because it is tethered to something that mattered deeply to us: trust, dignity, loyalty, justice.

We may carry a grudge against someone who betrayed us, humiliated us, excluded us, or hurt us without remorse. But we can also hold grudges against systems—institutions that failed us, workplaces that exploited us, communities that judged us. In these cases, the grudge becomes something bigger than personal hurt; it becomes a protest against patterns, power imbalances, and moral violations that transcend individual interaction.

Psychologically speaking, a grudge often serves a protective function. It preserves our memory of harm so that we do not place ourselves in similar situations again. It reminds us of who was unsafe, who failed us, who minimized our pain. The grudge becomes a signal—a moral boundary line reinforced by emotional memory. In this sense, it can be adaptive, even wise. But when it is left unchecked, unspoken, or unprocessed, it can also harden into something corrosive—resentment that leaks into unrelated areas of life, shaping how we see others and ourselves.

Let us also distinguish between a grudge and simple anger. Anger can flare in the moment and fade just as quickly. A grudge, on the other hand, remains. It does not require daily attention but can be triggered by a name, a smell, a voice, a place. Its persistence is not a sign of pettiness, but of emotional depth. We hold grudges not over trivialities, but over events that struck at our moral core.

The language we use to describe grudges often reflects cultural discomfort. We say someone is "stuck in the past" or "needs to let it go," as if time alone should heal all wounds. But time does not heal wounds that were never treated. And in the absence of repair, recognition, or sincere apology, the mind holds on—not out of vindictiveness, but out of justice-seeking.

Grudges are not only reactions to pain; they are responses to silence. A wound that was never witnessed, a betrayal that was never owned, an apology that never came—these are the conditions under which grudges form. And they are made stronger by every attempt to dismiss or minimize them. "You're overreacting." "That happened years ago." "You're too sensitive." Such words don't heal; they deepen the wound.

In many cases, the person holding the grudge is not hoping to punish the other. They are hoping to feel heard, understood, respected. But when that hope is repeatedly denied, the emotional injury becomes encrusted, encased in memory. The grudge becomes a monument to an unresolved story.

So what, then, is a grudge?

It is moral pain that has not found language.

It is loyalty to a violated boundary.

It is a refusal to pretend that everything is okay when it never was.

It is memory with meaning—and the desire for justice that memory protects.

This book is not written to tell you that your grudges are wrong or right. It is written to tell you that they are human. They are not evidence of your failure to forgive—they are evidence of your need to be understood.

In the chapters that follow, we will explore the psychological structure of resentment, the cultural pressures to forgive, and the ways in which grudges are linked to identity, trauma, and healing. But before we can transform the grudge, we must first understand it—not as a problem to be eradicated, but as a signal to be interpreted.

To begin with compassion, we must first listen to what our pain is trying to say.

Chapter 2: The Psychology of Resentment

Resentment is not merely an emotional reaction; it is a deeply layered psychological experience that weaves together memory, judgment, morality, and unmet needs. To understand the grudge, we must first understand resentment—not just as a feeling, but as a process.

At its core, resentment is a form of **moral outrage**—not explosive like anger, but simmering, enduring, and self-protective. It arises when we believe we have been wronged, when our expectations of fairness or dignity have been violated, and when those violations have not been acknowledged or rectified. Unlike anger, which is often immediate and visible, resentment tends to settle quietly in the psyche. It lodges itself in memory, reinforcing a sense of injustice and urging us not to forget.

The Emotional Anatomy of Resentment

Psychologists describe resentment as a **secondary emotion**, meaning it is often built upon more primary feelings like pain, fear, or disappointment. We feel hurt first—hurt by betrayal, rejection, neglect, humiliation. But when that hurt is denied, dismissed, or ignored, it transforms into something more guarded: resentment.

Resentment says: "You crossed a line, and no one noticed."

It says: "You took something from me, and I never got it back."

And sometimes it says: "You got away with it."

It is not a tantrum. It is a *moral protest.*

Resentment is not always loud, but it is always meaningful. It speaks on behalf of our boundaries, our unmet expectations, and our unhealed wounds. It is a survival mechanism that reminds us not to trust those who have harmed us—and it encourages us to avoid similar harm in the future. In this sense, resentment is not irrational. It is a **psychological defense**.

Cognitive Loops and Emotional Memory

Resentment is sustained not just by feeling, but by thought. The mind plays back the memory of the offense in a loop—revisiting details, replaying the conversations, reimagining how things could have gone differently. These loops are not simply emotional indulgences; they are the mind's effort to **make sense of what happened** and to resolve the incongruity between our moral expectations and the painful reality we experienced.

Neuroscience tells us that the brain treats social pain much like physical pain. The regions activated during emotional rejection, betrayal, or humiliation overlap with those triggered by physical injury. In other words, **resentment is not just metaphorically painful—it is biologically encoded as pain**.

This is why we cannot simply "get over it." The body remembers. The mind replays. The soul resists closure without meaning.

The Role of Injustice and Power

Resentment intensifies when the offense occurs within a context of power imbalance. A child resents a parent who never apologized. An employee resents a manager who misused authority. A partner resents being blamed for a dynamic they didn't create. In each of these, there is not just hurt—but **powerlessness**.

When we cannot express ourselves, when we are not allowed to defend our perspective, or when speaking up would risk further harm, resentment takes root in silence. It becomes our inner advocate, carrying the burden of unspoken truth.

Psychologically, this creates what researchers call a "**moral injury**"—a rupture in our internal value system that cannot be reconciled until justice is restored or reimagined. Without that reconciliation, we remain suspended in resentment, looping through the same thoughts and feelings, hoping for an outcome that never arrives.

Resentment as a Social Signal

Resentment does not occur in a vacuum. It thrives in relational systems—family, friendship, workplace, religious communities—where power, validation, and loyalty are always in play. In these systems, resentment often signals an **imbalance**: too much giving without receiving, too much compliance without recognition, too much silence when truth was needed.

From a psychological perspective, resentment is a relational flare—a signal that a bond has been broken, that a norm has been violated, or that the emotional labor has not been mutual. It is often the result of **unreciprocated effort**—emotional investment not returned.

And when that imbalance is denied or normalized by others, the person holding the resentment becomes further isolated. The emotional experience is invalidated, and the grudge deepens—not as an act of immaturity, but as a way to protect what little sense of fairness remains.

Shame, Guilt, and Self-Blame

Another layer of resentment is **internal conflict**. Many people feel ashamed of holding a grudge, especially when they've been conditioned to believe that forgiveness is the only moral response to harm. They may begin to question themselves: "Am I too sensitive? Am I making too much of this? Shouldn't I have moved on by now?"

This inner guilt compounds the pain. It suggests that not only were we hurt—but we are also wrong for still feeling hurt. This is where the grudge becomes heavy—not because of the original wound, but because of the psychological **burden of carrying it alone**.

In these moments, the grudge does not ask for revenge. It asks for **permission**—to feel, to speak, to be heard without being condemned. It asks for a space where moral injury can coexist with emotional honesty.

From Suppression to Awareness

Many people suppress their resentment, believing it is better to bury it than confront it. But repression does not resolve pain—it only delays its expression. Over time, suppressed resentment can manifest in indirect ways: sarcasm, avoidance, passive-aggression, withdrawal, even depression. The emotional charge finds a way to surface, even if the conscious mind resists.

What transforms resentment is not repression, but reflection. To become aware of our grudge is not to indulge it—it is to understand it. And when we understand it, we create the possibility of **agency**. We may not change the past, but we can choose how to carry it forward.

In Summary

Resentment is not weakness. It is the psyche's response to moral imbalance, emotional neglect, or unacknowledged harm. It is built on the architecture of thought, memory, and emotional logic. It is sustained by silence and resolved only through acknowledgment—whether that comes from others or from within ourselves.

In the next chapter, we will look more closely at what happens when **forgiveness fails**—when the social script urges us to move on, but the soul remains unresolved.

Because sometimes, the refusal to forgive is not spite.

It is self-preservation.

Chapter 3: When Forgiveness Fails

Forgiveness is often presented as a moral imperative—a necessary act for emotional healing and spiritual growth. We are told that forgiveness sets us free, that to forgive is to rise above our pain, and that holding onto resentment only poisons the soul. This message is echoed in religious texts, psychological advice columns, and motivational speeches. And yet, despite all the pressure to forgive, many people cannot. Or do not. Or try to—only to find that the pain still lingers.

What happens when forgiveness fails?

What happens when the words "I forgive you" feel hollow, forced, or untrue?

What happens when the desire to let go collides with the reality of a wound that hasn't healed?

These questions are not signs of weakness. They are signs of depth—of a psyche that refuses to rush emotional resolution, of a heart that knows the difference between superficial peace and authentic healing. When forgiveness fails, it is not because we are too angry or too bitter. It is often because the conditions for real forgiveness were never met.

The Myth of Instant Forgiveness

In popular culture and spiritual circles, forgiveness is sometimes framed as an act that can be accomplished in a single moment—a switch to be flipped, a feeling to be summoned. But true forgiveness is rarely that simple. It is a process, not a performance. It requires safety, recognition, and often, remorse. Without these elements, the expectation to forgive can feel coercive, even violent.

People are often told to "just forgive and forget," as if memory itself is a moral flaw. But forgiveness without memory is not healing; it is suppression. And forgiveness without accountability is not grace; it is erasure.

Forgiveness fails when it is rushed.

It fails when it is demanded.

It fails when it becomes a tool for silence, rather than truth.

The Social Pressure to Forgive

We live in a society that values appearances—peace over conflict, resolution over ambiguity. This creates a pressure to forgive even when the hurt runs deep and the harm continues. Survivors of abuse are asked to forgive their abusers. Marginalized communities are urged to move on from historical injustices. Victims of betrayal are told to take the high road.

But forgiveness, when demanded, becomes another form of control. It shifts the moral burden away from the offender and onto the injured. It places the responsibility of healing on the one who was harmed.

This pressure is especially acute in religious and spiritual contexts, where forgiveness is often equated with righteousness. And while many faith traditions do hold forgiveness as a virtue, they also emphasize justice, truth, and repentance. To forgive without these is not spiritual transcendence—it is emotional denial.

Apology and the Absence of Accountability

Forgiveness is often tied to the presence—or absence—of an apology. A sincere apology can open the door to healing. But what if the apology never comes? What if the person who hurt you refuses to admit it? What if they apologize without taking responsibility, or worse, manipulate the apology into another form of harm?

Many people feel stuck in their resentment not because they want to be angry, but because the apology they hoped for never arrived. Or because the apology that did arrive was a performance: "I'm sorry you feel that way" rather than "I'm sorry for what I did."

An apology that lacks ownership is worse than none at all—it adds insult to injury. It tells the injured that their feelings are the problem, not the original offense. In such cases, the failure to forgive is not moral weakness. It is **moral clarity**.

Forgiveness as Silence

When forgiveness is expected in the absence of justice, it becomes a form of silence. It asks the injured to bury their pain in order to preserve someone else's comfort. This kind of forgiveness does not bring healing; it brings

disconnection—from the self, from truth, and from the emotional reality of what happened.

Many people who force themselves to forgive prematurely end up feeling more wounded, not less. They doubt their instincts. They question their worth. They feel guilt not just for what happened, but for how long it hurts. This is the emotional cost of false forgiveness.

The Desire to Forgive vs. The Readiness to Forgive

There is often a gap between the desire to forgive and the readiness to forgive. A person may long for peace, may genuinely want to move on—but their heart is not ready. The trauma is too fresh. The trust is too broken. The apology is too shallow—or missing altogether.

This is where forgiveness fails—not because the person is resistant, but because the emotional soil has not been prepared. Forgiveness, like healing, requires time. And sometimes, what we call a grudge is simply the space between injury and readiness.

It is not wrong to occupy that space.

It is not wrong to linger in that pause.

It is not wrong to say: "I want to forgive, but I'm not there yet."

When Not Forgiving Is the Healthier Option

In some cases, forgiveness may not be possible—or even desirable. If the harm was severe, if the offender remains dangerous, or if the act of forgiving would require the victim to minimize their truth, then holding on to a grudge may be an act of **self-preservation**.

Not all pain needs to be forgiven.

Not all offenses deserve reconciliation.

Not all journeys lead to release.

Sometimes, clarity is more important than closure.

Sometimes, boundaries are more healing than bridges.

Sometimes, holding on is the most honest thing we can do.

In Summary

Forgiveness is a powerful force, but it is not a universal requirement. It must be freely given, not socially demanded. It must arise from truth, not obligation. And it must honor the pain it seeks to release.

When forgiveness fails, it does not mean we are broken. It means we are still healing. It means our pain deserves time, space, and witness. And it means that sometimes, the most compassionate act is not letting go—but listening.

In the next chapter, we will explore what that pain is trying to say—how our resentment speaks through the need for **justice, closure, and the desire to be heard**.

Chapter 4: Justice, Closure, and the Need to Be Heard

Behind every unresolved hurt, behind every quietly carried grudge, there is a story that longs to be heard. Not just a retelling of events, but a moral account—a plea for recognition, fairness, and emotional truth. If forgiveness is about letting go, then resentment is about *holding on until justice is done.* And often, justice begins with simply being heard.

Contrary to popular belief, most people who hold grudges are not seeking revenge. They are seeking **validation**—the kind of validation that says, "What happened to you matters." "You didn't imagine it." "You're not wrong for feeling this way." These statements do not erase the pain, but they allow it to exist in the light, rather than fester in silence.

We cannot talk about forgiveness or closure without talking about justice. Because for many, what looks like a grudge is actually a form of justice-seeking in a world that too often tells the hurt to stay quiet.

The Moral Logic of Justice

When something unjust happens—betrayal, abuse, humiliation, neglect—it violates our sense of how the world *should* work. Our inner compass expects fairness. When that expectation is shattered, our mind searches for a way to restore order.

This is the foundation of justice: the idea that wrongs should be righted, that harm should be acknowledged, and that consequences should follow misconduct. Without justice, the injured party feels disoriented—not just emotionally, but morally. The grudge becomes a signal that the story is unfinished.

People often think that forgiveness will bring closure, but closure without justice is an illusion. It asks the wounded to move on while the story remains incomplete, while the pain remains unseen, while the person responsible continues unaccountable.

This doesn't mean we seek punishment in every case. But we do seek meaning. We seek repair. We seek acknowledgment.

The Role of Acknowledgment

If justice is the framework, **acknowledgment is its emotional core.**

Acknowledgment does not require legal systems or public spectacles. It simply means facing the truth without minimizing it. It is saying: "Yes, that happened. Yes, it hurt. Yes, I understand why you're still affected."

This is why so many grudges persist—not because people are angry by nature, but because their pain was met with denial, indifference, or deflection. "It wasn't that bad." "I didn't mean to." "Why are you bringing that up again?" These responses don't just dismiss the event—they *erase the person's emotional experience of it.*

When acknowledgment is withheld, the wound deepens. The grudge strengthens. And the one holding it begins to feel invisible, even crazy, for needing justice in a world that only wants them to forgive and forget.

The Myth of Closure

Closure is another concept wrapped in illusion. We speak of closure as if it's a door that neatly shuts once we've processed our pain. But closure is not a single moment. It is not an apology. It is not even the end of a relationship or conversation. Closure is a process of meaning-making.

True closure occurs not when the story is rewritten, but when it is **fully told.** When we can speak our truth and be received—not fixed, not debated, just received. When we can grieve what was lost, mourn what will never be, and still choose how to carry it forward.

Some stories will never receive external justice. The apology won't come. The offender won't change. The wrong won't be made right. In these cases, closure can only be found **internally**—by honoring our experience, by giving ourselves the recognition we were denied, and by refusing to gaslight ourselves into silence.

This is not the same as "getting over it." It is **getting clear** about what happened, what it cost, and what it still means.

Why Being Heard Matters

There is a profound psychological and emotional need to be heard. To tell our story. To have someone bear witness without judgment, interruption, or justification. This need is not petty—it is **primal.**

Being heard affirms our reality. It restores dignity. It tells us we are not alone. In trauma studies, researchers emphasize that *telling the story in a safe space* is often a key step toward healing. But many people never get that opportunity. Their stories are dismissed, their truth questioned, and their feelings invalidated.

The result? The grudge becomes the only surviving proof that something happened. It becomes the emotional archive of an unresolved moral wound. And until someone—anyone—truly listens, the grudge remains.

Justice Is Not Always Punishment

It is important to clarify that justice is not always about punishment. It is about **restoration**. It is about naming what was broken, understanding its impact, and seeking some form of repair—emotional, relational, or spiritual.

In some cases, justice is simply being believed.

In others, it is an apology that takes responsibility.

Sometimes, it is creating new boundaries to protect one's peace.

And sometimes, it is walking away from the person or system that caused the harm—because staying would mean betraying yourself.

What justice looks like will vary for each person and each wound. But without justice, closure is counterfeit, and forgiveness becomes a performance instead of a process.

In Summary

At the heart of many grudges lies a longing—for justice, for acknowledgment, for the basic human dignity of being heard. These are not small things. They are the building blocks of trust, meaning, and peace.

To dismiss a grudge without listening to its message is to ignore the moral wound it protects. And to push forgiveness without understanding the underlying need for justice is to place emotional convenience above human truth.

In the next chapter, we will explore how these moral wounds shape not only our emotions—but our very sense of **self.** Because a grudge is never just about what happened. It is also about who we became in the aftermath.

Chapter 5: Grudges and Identity

To understand the depth and persistence of a grudge, we must look beyond the incident that caused it. A grudge is not just about the past—it's also about who we are now. It is not only a memory of what was done to us; it is a statement about who we became as a result.

Grudges are not simply emotional leftovers. They become part of our identity. They live not just in our memory, but in our worldview, our sense of self, and the stories we tell about our lives. To let go of a grudge is not only to release a feeling—it is, in some cases, to question the shape our lives took because of it.

This chapter explores the deep entanglement between grudges and identity—how resentment shapes our self-perception, how it can define our values and relationships, and how it can sometimes become the last remaining marker of a boundary once crossed.

When the Hurt Becomes Part of the Self

When we are deeply wronged—especially by someone close to us—the impact goes beyond pain. It can destabilize our sense of self. We begin to ask, "Why did this happen to me?" or "What does this say about who I am?"

The brain tries to make sense of the violation. In doing so, it weaves the story of that experience into our ongoing identity. We don't just remember what happened—we begin to live in relation to it.

The person who was betrayed becomes "the one who cannot trust."

The person who was abandoned becomes "the one who must never need anyone."

The person who was silenced becomes "the one who must speak out at all costs."

These are not just coping mechanisms—they become **identity markers**. And the grudge becomes the emotional glue that holds that identity together.

The Risk of Letting Go

Because a grudge can become part of how we define ourselves, letting go of it can feel deeply unsettling. It may feel like losing a piece of who we are—a piece that kept us safe, that helped us make sense of our pain, that allowed us to remember who crossed our boundary.

This is one reason people resist letting go, even when they want to. It's not just about forgiveness—it's about **self-preservation**.

Letting go of a grudge can raise difficult questions:

- "Who am I if I'm no longer angry?"
- "What will protect me if I stop remembering?"
- "Will I become vulnerable again if I let this go?"
- "If I forgive, does that mean it didn't matter?"

These are not trivial concerns. They reflect the profound psychological investment that can accompany long-held resentment. In some cases, the grudge becomes the only consistent part of our narrative in a chaotic or unjust story.

The Role of Betrayal in Identity Formation

Betrayal, in particular, cuts into the very heart of identity. It doesn't just hurt—it redefines. When someone we trusted harms us, it calls into question our judgment, our worth, our ability to discern danger. This psychological rupture leaves a residue that can shape the way we relate to others—and to ourselves—for years.

Many people respond by developing protective identities:

- The lone wolf who no longer depends on anyone
- The advocate who fights for others because no one fought for them
- The skeptic who questions sincerity and stays two steps ahead of disappointment

These identities are not inherently negative. In fact, they often reflect strength, insight, and resilience. But when they are built entirely around a wound, they can harden into armor that keeps others—and healing—at a distance.

Grudges and Moral Identity

Some grudges are not about emotional harm alone—they are about **moral injury**. When we are treated unjustly, and no one acknowledges it, our grudge becomes a moral stance. It says, "This was wrong. I refuse to pretend otherwise." In these cases, the grudge serves not as a blockage, but as a **moral anchor**.

To relinquish the grudge would feel like betraying oneself, or like abandoning the truth of what happened. The resentment becomes an assertion of dignity, especially when no one else stood up in our defense.

This is why telling someone to "just let it go" can be so damaging. It ignores the moral identity embedded in the pain. It turns a deeply ethical experience into an emotional flaw.

Resentment as Resistance

In oppressive contexts—where people are silenced, marginalized, or exploited—grudges can become acts of **resistance**. They are a way of preserving the memory of injustice when the world wants it erased.

Think of the activist who refuses to forget the crimes of history.

Or the survivor who refuses to pretend the abuse never happened.

Or the citizen who won't move on from corruption, brutality, or systemic violence.

These are not petty grudges—they are **conscious refusals** to allow truth to be buried. In such cases, resentment is not a prison—it is a posture of remembrance and defiance.

Reclaiming Identity from the Grudge

While grudges can become part of our identity, they do not have to **define** it. It is possible to honor our pain, to remember our story, and still choose a fuller, freer self beyond the wound.

This begins with **separating the story from the self**. We can say:

- "This happened to me, but it is not the only thing that defines me."
- "I was wronged, and that matters—but I am more than what they did."
- "I remember because it shaped me, not because it owns me."

In this way, we reclaim our identity not through forgetting, but through reframing. We keep the story, but we write the next chapter with conscious agency.

Letting go of a grudge, then, does not mean erasing the self-protection it gave us. It means recognizing that we have grown strong enough to protect ourselves in new ways—that we no longer need pain to remember our worth.

In Summary

Grudges often form at the intersection of harm and identity. They are not just reactions to what was done to us—they are responses to how those events reshaped us. When we understand how closely our resentment is tied to our self-concept, we gain clarity about why letting go is so hard—and why it must be approached with care, not pressure.

Healing is not forgetting. And forgiveness is not the erasure of moral memory. It is the slow, conscious reclaiming of a self that deserves more than just survival.

In the next chapter, we will look at how grudges play out in our **closest relationships**—where trust, love, and silence often collide.

Chapter 6: Grudges in Relationships

Of all the places grudges can take root, the most fertile—and the most painful—ground is our closest relationships. Family, romantic partners, friendships—these are the spaces where trust is highest, expectations are deepest, and vulnerability is most exposed. When betrayal or emotional neglect occurs within these bonds, the wound cuts deeper. And often, it is not the initial pain that hurts the most—it is the silence that follows.

Grudges in relationships are not always loud. Sometimes, they are quiet, passive, invisible to outsiders but deeply felt within. They sit beneath years of conversation, tension, smiles, and polite dinners. They manifest as avoidance, sarcasm, defensiveness, or the inability to say what really needs to be said. In time, they become part of the relationship's emotional architecture.

In this chapter, we explore how grudges form and function within personal relationships, why they are so difficult to confront, and what it means to either heal them—or live honestly with their presence.

The Hidden Currency of Emotional Expectations

Every relationship is shaped by unspoken agreements—expectations of loyalty, honesty, reciprocity, and emotional safety. These agreements may never be explicitly stated, but they are deeply felt. When one party violates these expectations, especially repeatedly or without remorse, a grudge often forms in the silence that follows.

The friend who shared your secret.

The partner who emotionally withdrew.

The sibling who always took and never gave.

The parent who saw your pain but said nothing.

In these cases, resentment often builds gradually—not from a single event, but from a pattern of unmet emotional needs. The grudge, then, becomes a ledger of those unmet moments—a history of what was not given or not acknowledged.

Family Grudges: The Unresolved Past in the Present

Family grudges are among the most complex. They are shaped not just by behavior, but by identity. Our earliest ideas of safety, fairness, and love are formed within the family unit. When a parent fails to protect, a sibling betrays, or a relative shows favoritism, the emotional injury often echoes into adulthood.

What makes family grudges particularly challenging is the **social script** around family unity. We are told to "love them anyway," to "let bygones be bygones," or that "they did the best they could." These narratives, however well-intentioned, can invalidate legitimate pain. And when the person hurt is not allowed to speak their truth, the grudge solidifies—not out of malice, but out of unacknowledged moral injury.

In many families, grudges are not openly discussed but passed down like emotional heirlooms. The silence becomes generational. The emotional tone of gatherings is tense but polite. And beneath the surface, everyone knows who has never forgiven—and who has never apologized.

Romantic Grudges: When Intimacy Becomes Injury

In romantic relationships, grudges often stem from emotional betrayals—lies, broken promises, infidelity, or neglect. But more often than not, they form through **accumulated hurt**: emotional dismissals, unresolved arguments, feelings of being unheard or undervalued.

A partner might say, "You're always angry," without realizing that years of emotional neglect created that anger. They may focus on the expression of resentment without acknowledging the experiences that generated it.

In such cases, the grudge becomes a substitute for the conversation that never happened. It is the emotional residue of words swallowed, boundaries crossed, and needs ignored. Over time, it replaces intimacy with guardedness.

If left unaddressed, grudges in romantic partnerships create emotional distance. They erode the foundation of trust and become barriers to real connection. The irony is that the person we once felt safest with now feels emotionally dangerous—not because they always hurt us, but because they once did and never truly owned it.

Friendships and the Unspoken Grudge

Friendships are built on mutual care, loyalty, and shared experiences. But when imbalance creeps in—when one friend becomes emotionally unavailable, repeatedly cancels plans, or only reaches out when they need something—a grudge can take form quietly.

Unlike family or romantic relationships, where confrontation may be expected, friendships are more fragile in terms of structure. Confronting a friend about a grudge can feel like a risk to the entire relationship. As a result, many people **withdraw rather than confront**, letting the friendship slowly fade while carrying resentment beneath the surface.

Sometimes, the grudge emerges not from what a friend did, but from what they didn't do: not showing up in times of need, not defending us in a moment of vulnerability, not acknowledging their absence when it mattered most.

Passive-Aggression and the Disguised Grudge

Grudges in relationships rarely announce themselves directly. Instead, they often disguise themselves in subtle behaviors:

- Sarcasm in place of vulnerability
- Withholding affection or praise
- Making jokes that contain hidden jabs
- Avoiding conflict while secretly stewing

These are not just communication failures. They are defense mechanisms. The person holding the grudge may feel too unsafe to express it directly—or may have tried and been dismissed. In such cases, passive-aggression becomes the only remaining outlet.

But these disguised expressions of resentment rarely bring healing. Instead, they erode trust, sow confusion, and deepen the emotional distance. The unspoken grudge becomes a fog that dims the clarity of the relationship.

Confronting or Living With the Grudge

Not all grudges in relationships can—or should—be resolved. Some require confrontation, mutual ownership, and honest conversation. Others may persist because the other party remains defensive, oblivious, or unwilling to engage. In these situations, the person holding the grudge must make a difficult choice: confront it, carry it, or release it privately.

Each path comes with trade-offs:

- **Confrontation** offers potential healing but carries emotional risk.
- **Carrying it** preserves boundaries but may limit closeness.
- **Releasing it privately** allows for internal peace but requires self-validation.

There is no single right answer. What matters most is that the decision is **conscious**, not forced. That we stop pretending everything is fine when it's not. That we honor our pain without letting it harden into permanent isolation.

In Summary

Grudges in relationships are not evidence of emotional weakness. They are the echo of unresolved connection, the memory of love gone unattended, and the moral protest of the unacknowledged.

To navigate these grudges, we must learn to listen—to ourselves, to each other, and to the stories our pain is telling. We must dare to name what was broken, even if it was in the name of love. And we must accept that sometimes, honesty—not harmony—is what relationships need most.

In the next chapter, we'll broaden our view beyond the personal and into the **cultural and religious dimensions** of grudges—where morality, forgiveness, and social expectations intersect in powerful and often conflicting ways.

Chapter 7: Cultural and Religious Views on Grudges

Across cultures and spiritual traditions, there is perhaps no moral theme more universally emphasized than forgiveness. From sermons and sacred texts to literature and folklore, the message is clear: to forgive is noble. To hold a grudge is spiritually, morally, and socially suspect.

And yet, across time and geography, human beings continue to carry resentment. We remember. We grieve. We resist forgetting. Why?

Because cultural ideals do not always align with lived reality. Because religious teachings are sometimes misinterpreted, oversimplified, or used to silence necessary truth. And because the human heart, in all its complexity, is not governed solely by dogma—it is shaped by experience, pain, memory, and longing for justice.

In this chapter, we examine the complicated landscape of cultural and religious teachings on forgiveness and resentment. We explore the tension between moral aspiration and emotional reality, and the ways in which some cultures and faiths hold space for nuance—while others suppress it.

Forgiveness as a Moral Ideal

Nearly all major world religions teach forgiveness as a central virtue:

- **Christianity** emphasizes unconditional forgiveness, as embodied in the teachings of Jesus: "Forgive seventy times seven." The Lord's Prayer itself ties divine forgiveness to our willingness to forgive others.
- **Islam** encourages mercy and pardon as noble traits. The Qur'an calls believers to forgive, reminding them that "forgiveness is better" (Surah Al-Baqarah 2:237), while also recognizing the legitimacy of justice and restitution.
- **Judaism** sees forgiveness as a process grounded in teshuvah (repentance), which requires the wrongdoer to genuinely atone before forgiveness can be given. Forgiveness is encouraged but not blindly mandated.

- **Buddhism** views forgiveness as a path toward inner peace and liberation from suffering. Letting go of resentment is seen as a release of attachment and ego.
- **Hinduism** also teaches kṣamā (forgiveness) as a divine quality, necessary for spiritual growth, yet acknowledges karma and the need for accountability.

These traditions, while often quoted to promote universal forgiveness, actually offer a much more **layered** and **conditional** understanding of resentment and reconciliation than is popularly understood.

When Forgiveness Is Forced

In many cultures, forgiveness is not just recommended—it is expected. This expectation often turns forgiveness from a spiritual path into a **social obligation**, especially for those in less powerful positions: women, children, marginalized communities, and survivors of abuse.

Religious or cultural pressures can be weaponized to suppress dissent. Victims are told to forgive in order to be virtuous. To stay silent in order to preserve family unity. To let go in order to avoid "sinning" themselves.

But when forgiveness is coerced, it ceases to be spiritual. It becomes another act of **emotional control.**

In this way, well-meaning teachings on compassion are sometimes used to protect the reputations of abusers or to preserve toxic hierarchies. The grudge, then, becomes not a failure of the soul—but a shield for the truth.

Honor, Shame, and Collective Memory

In **honor-based cultures**, the concept of grudge-holding takes on a unique form. A family's reputation may depend on how it handles betrayal or disrespect. In such cultures, forgiveness may be perceived as weakness, and retaliation as a form of justice.

In **shame-based cultures**, where appearance and conformity matter deeply, grudges may be hidden but deeply felt. The public face shows forgiveness, but the private self remembers everything. Appearances are preserved, but healing is often delayed or denied.

In **collectivist societies**, where the group's harmony is prioritized over individual expression, people may suppress resentment to maintain peace. But this suppression doesn't erase the emotional wound—it simply buries it under obligation.

Contrast this with **individualistic cultures**, which often encourage open confrontation and "moving on" through self-help narratives. Here, grudges may be pathologized as a sign of personal weakness or lack of emotional intelligence, rather than understood in their full social and moral context.

Neither cultural approach is perfect. In both, the complexity of resentment can be lost.

Sacred Space for Complexity

Despite social and institutional pressures, many spiritual and cultural traditions do contain space for complexity. In the deeper layers of religious philosophy, there is often an unspoken acknowledgment that **forgiveness without justice is incomplete**.

For instance:

- In Judaism, forgiveness is not required unless the offender has sought forgiveness sincerely. The Talmud teaches that a person should try to make amends up to three times—but if forgiveness is not given, the guilt is transferred.
- In Islam, divine forgiveness is vast, but interpersonal forgiveness is conditional upon acknowledgment and repair.
- In Christianity, the parable of the unforgiving servant is not a blanket command to forgive without reflection—it is a critique of hypocrisy, not an invalidation of pain.
- In Buddhism, anger is not a sin—it is suffering. The goal is to understand its roots, not to shame its presence.

These teachings reveal a deeper truth: spiritual maturity does not mean erasing emotion. It means engaging with it honestly, mindfully, and with compassion for the self and others.

The Cultural Shame of Holding On

Across many societies, people feel ashamed for holding on to pain. They ask themselves:

- "Why can't I forgive?"
- "Am I a bad person for still being angry?"
- "What's wrong with me that I can't move on?"

These questions are not just psychological—they are **cultural scripts**. They reflect the internalization of a moral narrative that says healing must look like release, even when release is premature or impossible.

In truth, the shame of holding on is often **more damaging than the grudge itself**. It adds guilt to pain. It isolates the sufferer further. And it prevents people from exploring the deeper messages their resentment may be carrying.

Embracing Emotional Integrity

The spiritual ideal of forgiveness should never come at the cost of **emotional integrity**. True forgiveness is not the suppression of truth—it is its integration. It is the moment when pain is fully seen, honored, and re-contextualized within a wider understanding.

For many, the path toward peace does not begin with letting go. It begins with **permission to feel**. To grieve. To speak. To stop pretending.

The goal is not to rid ourselves of all resentment, but to **befriend the parts of us that still hurt**, so we may listen with kindness—and act with intention.

In Summary

Culture and religion shape how we view grudges—but not always in ways that honor the full emotional and moral landscape. While teachings on forgiveness offer valuable wisdom, they must be applied with nuance, empathy, and attention to power dynamics.

Sometimes, holding on is not resistance to growth—it is **the beginning of it**.

In the next chapter, we will explore how to distinguish between **healthy and toxic grudges**—how to know when holding on is protecting us, and when it is harming us.

Chapter 8: Healthy vs. Toxic Grudges

To some, the idea of a "healthy grudge" may seem contradictory. Culturally, grudges are almost always framed in negative terms—unforgiving, bitter, destructive. But not all grudges are toxic. Some are *honest*. Some are *necessary*. Some protect us from further harm. The challenge is not to eliminate all grudges, but to learn how to **discern** between those that serve us and those that sabotage us.

In this chapter, we explore what makes a grudge healthy, when it becomes toxic, and how to recognize the tipping point between **moral memory** and **emotional stagnation**.

The Protective Grudge

A healthy grudge is not a sign of pettiness—it's a **signal of emotional integrity**. It reflects a moment when your boundaries were violated and your need for respect or justice went unmet. Instead of denying the impact, the healthy grudge *holds space* for it.

This kind of grudge:

- Protects you from re-engaging with unsafe people.
- Reminds you of your values and self-worth.
- Allows you to maintain healthy distance without needing revenge.
- Signals a part of your story that shaped you, but doesn't define you.

A protective grudge keeps the memory alive not to relive pain—but to ensure that the lesson isn't forgotten. It honors your experience without controlling your future.

This is not resentment as a weapon. It is **resentment as wisdom**.

Signs of a Healthy Grudge

- You are aware of why you feel the way you do.
- You have reflected on the experience and can express it without spiraling.

- You use the memory to inform your choices—not to punish others.
- You feel emotionally safer because of the boundaries it upholds.
- You don't feel consumed or poisoned by the grudge—you feel *clearer*.

A healthy grudge is like scar tissue: a visible reminder of pain that healed imperfectly, but left behind a form of protection. It marks the site of growth and survival—not ongoing decay.

The Descent into Toxicity

In contrast, a **toxic grudge** is one that begins to erode your peace of mind, your ability to trust, and your relationships with others. It is no longer about self-protection—it becomes self-imprisonment. It festers, distorts, and fuels cycles of blame, obsession, or retribution.

Toxic grudges are often the result of unresolved emotional pain that has not been examined—pain that becomes the lens through which we see everything and everyone.

Over time, toxic grudges can:

- Distort your sense of reality.
- Make you cynical or emotionally numb.
- Lead you to assume ill intent even when none exists.
- Reinforce feelings of victimhood at the expense of growth.
- Sabotage new opportunities or healthy relationships.

Rather than keeping you safe, toxic resentment **keeps you stuck**—locked in a past moment that no longer serves you, even if it once did.

Signs of a Toxic Grudge

- The emotional intensity remains high, even after significant time has passed.
- You find yourself replaying the event obsessively.
- You speak about the incident with hostility or contempt.
- You derive identity or superiority from the grudge.
- You find it hard to empathize with others because of your pain.

- The grudge affects your ability to enjoy new relationships or experiences.

Toxic grudges tend to **inflate the offender and shrink the self**. They give the person who hurt you ongoing power in your emotional life. They keep you tethered to someone or something that no longer deserves access to your mind or heart.

Why We Cling to the Toxic Grudge

Even when we know a grudge is hurting us, we may find it difficult to let go. This is often because:

- **The grudge gives meaning to pain.** Letting go may feel like the offense is forgotten or minimized.
- **The grudge provides structure.** In a world that feels unjust, it offers a sense of moral order.
- **The grudge protects us from vulnerability.** Releasing it might require confronting grief, fear, or lost hope.

Sometimes, we cling to a toxic grudge because the alternative feels even more frightening: facing the wound beneath it. In this way, resentment becomes a defense against deeper sorrow.

But the longer we hold a grudge that no longer serves us, the more it becomes a **barrier to healing.** It keeps us emotionally aligned with people and events we no longer need.

Moving from Toxic to Healthy

Not all toxic grudges need to be released entirely. Some can be **transformed**. With awareness, compassion, and intentional reflection, a toxic grudge can become a healthy boundary, a clear lesson, or a stepping stone toward deeper self-understanding.

Here's how the shift might look:

Toxic Grudge	Healthy Alternative
Obsessing over the past	Reflecting with purpose
Wishing for revenge	Seeking growth or distance
Feeling morally superior	Feeling morally clear
Internalizing bitterness	Externalizing lessons learned
Letting the offender live rent-free in your mind	Reclaiming emotional space

The key is not to erase what happened—but to reclaim your agency in how you carry it forward.

The Role of Self-Compassion

One of the most powerful tools in shifting a grudge from toxic to healthy is **self-compassion**. It allows us to hold our pain gently, without shame. It reminds us that struggling to let go doesn't make us weak—it makes us human.

Self-compassion tells us:

- "It makes sense that this hurt you."
- "You did what you needed to survive."
- "You are allowed to carry this as long as you need."
- "And when you're ready, you'll know how to carry it differently."

There is no timeline for healing. But there is a turning point—a moment when we realize we are carrying more than we need, and that our story deserves more than bitterness.

In Summary

Not all grudges are harmful. Some are the soul's attempt to preserve truth. Others are the psyche's way of keeping us safe. But when a grudge begins to poison our peace, cloud our judgment, or isolate us from others, it is time to listen—not to silence it, but to understand it more deeply.

Resentment can be a teacher. But eventually, we must decide whether it still belongs in the classroom of our lives.

In the next chapter, we explore one of the most powerful dynamics behind grudges: **power**—who has it, who loses it, and how resentment becomes a response to being silenced, controlled, or disempowered.

Chapter 9: Grudges and Power

At its core, every grudge tells a story—not just of pain, but of power. The power someone had to hurt us. The power they misused. The power we lost in the aftermath. The power we are still trying to reclaim.

Whether rooted in personal betrayal, systemic injustice, or quiet acts of emotional neglect, many grudges originate in moments when we were made to feel **small, silenced, or powerless**. These are not just emotional wounds; they are power imbalances frozen in memory.

In this chapter, we explore how power dynamics—between individuals, within families, across institutions, and throughout society—shape the grudges we hold, why they linger, and what they demand from us emotionally and morally.

Power Is More Than Control

Power in relationships is not always about dominance. It is also about **voice**, **agency**, and **impact**. We feel powerful when we are heard, respected, and seen. We feel powerless when our truth is ignored, our pain is minimized, or our boundaries are crossed without consequence.

A grudge often forms when:

- Someone had the power to hurt us, and did.
- We had no power to stop it, and no one intervened.
- The person who caused the harm never acknowledged it, and moved on freely.

In such cases, resentment becomes a **moral reaction** to that imbalance—a reminder that something was taken from us, and the scales were never reset.

The Resentment of the Voiceless

There is a unique kind of grudge born not from what was done—but from what was denied: the right to speak, to protest, to be taken seriously.

Children who were told to stay quiet.

Partners who were gaslit into self-doubt.

Employees whose concerns were dismissed.

Citizens whose rights were violated.

The common thread in these experiences is the absence of voice. In the silence that follows, the grudge becomes the only way the injured can still feel connected to what happened. It becomes the internal protest in a world that refused to listen.

In this sense, **grudges restore internal balance** when external justice is impossible. They give the hurt person a sense of moral continuity in the face of emotional erasure.

Power and the Inability to Apologize

One of the most overlooked reasons grudges persist is the offender's refusal—or inability—to apologize. In many cases, those who hurt us cling to their power by denying our reality. They fear that to admit fault is to lose control, respect, or moral standing.

Ironically, **refusing to acknowledge harm is itself an abuse of power**. It places emotional labor on the injured party. It demands that they "move on" without the restoration of dignity. And it prolongs the imbalance that created the grudge in the first place.

In such contexts, the grudge is not just about the original harm—it's about the **ongoing injustice of not being believed, not being valued, not being restored**.

Social Power and Collective Resentment

Grudges are not only personal—they are also **collective**. Entire communities and cultures carry the weight of injustice across generations.

- Descendants of enslaved people.
- Survivors of colonization and genocide.
- Marginalized groups to systemic discrimination.

These are not "grudges" in the petty sense—they are **historical memories of stolen power**. They are not easily "forgiven," because the conditions that caused them have often not changed.

When a society urges collective amnesia instead of collective healing, it breeds deeper resentment. People are not angry because they cannot let go. They are angry because the harm continues—and the narrative is still controlled by those who caused or benefited from it.

Resentment as a Form of Control

While many grudges form from being disempowered, it's also important to recognize that **grudges can become tools of control** themselves—especially in toxic dynamics.

In some relationships, a person may weaponize their grudge to manipulate others, guilt them into submission, or justify unkind behavior. In these cases, the grudge is no longer about truth or justice—it's about **retaining power over another**.

This is where grudges become morally complicated. They can begin as valid responses to injustice but evolve into cycles of harm if not examined carefully.

The challenge, then, is to ask:

- Is this grudge still protecting me—or is it controlling others?
- Is it about restoring fairness—or preserving resentment?

Reclaiming Internal Power

The most profound shift in any grudge narrative is the **reclamation of personal power**. This does not mean confronting the person who hurt you (though it might). It does not mean seeking revenge or forcing closure.

It means this: **refusing to let someone else's actions dictate your ongoing emotional truth**.

You reclaim your power when you stop waiting for an apology to validate your pain.

You reclaim your power when you choose who gets access to your life.

You reclaim your power when you let go—not because you were told to, but because you're ready.

You reclaim your power when your story no longer hinges on theirs.

Power Without Vengeance

Some people fear that reclaiming power means becoming cold, hard, or vindictive. But power reclaimed with **intention and reflection** does not make us harsh—it makes us whole.

It says:

- "You hurt me, and I remember."
- "But I will not center you in my story forever."
- "My power was never yours to take—it just took time for me to recognize it again."

This is not denial. It is not forced forgiveness. It is **mature self-restoration.**

In Summary

Grudges often form in the space where power was taken, denied, or abused. They are emotional records of that imbalance. To understand our resentment is to understand our relationship to power—both what we lost and what we are reclaiming.

Resentment can bind us to old hierarchies. But it can also wake us up to the possibility of living from a place of strength, agency, and truth.

In the next chapter, we explore what it means to walk the path toward peace—even when forgiveness is not possible. Because healing is not always about letting go. Sometimes, it's about **living with pain in a new way**.

Chapter 10: The Road to Peace (Even Without Forgiveness)

Forgiveness is often portrayed as the final destination of emotional healing. It's the moment when we rise above, let go, release the weight, and finally exhale. But for many people, that moment never comes—at least not in the way they were taught to expect it. And yet, they still heal. They still grow. They still find peace.

The truth is, **peace and forgiveness are not the same**. They are not synonymous, and they are not sequential. You can find peace even if forgiveness never arrives. You can feel whole even if you still carry a scar. And you can reclaim your life without pretending to forget what happened.

In this chapter, we explore what healing looks like **outside** of forgiveness—how people live, love, and evolve without resolving their pain through absolution. We examine what it means to shift from emotional reaction to emotional wisdom, and how peace, unlike forgiveness, does not always require reconciliation.

Peace Is Not the Absence of Pain

One of the most common misconceptions about peace is that it requires forgetting, numbing, or erasing what happened. But peace is not the elimination of pain—it is the **integration** of it.

You do not find peace by pretending the wound never existed. You find peace by accepting the wound's presence—and learning how to live around it, with it, beyond it.

Peace says:

- "This happened, and it hurt."
- "It mattered, and it still matters."
- "But it no longer controls me."
- "I can hold the memory without being consumed by it."

Forgiveness may or may not follow. But peace begins with *honesty*.

Emotional Clarity vs. Emotional Resolution

What we often seek is not forgiveness, but **emotional clarity**—the ability to understand what happened, name it truthfully, and decide what we want to do with that truth.

Clarity sounds like:

- "I was wronged, and I don't need to minimize that."
- "I still feel hurt, but I no longer need revenge."
- "I don't forgive you, but I release your control over my story."
- "You don't need to be in my life for me to find peace."

This kind of clarity allows us to move forward without reconciliation. It respects our emotions without being ruled by them.

In contrast, emotional resolution—the full sense of being healed, whole, and ready to forgive—might never come. And that's okay. Life does not require total resolution for forward movement. It only requires *movement.*

Letting Go Without Letting Them Back In

A major obstacle to peace is the false belief that letting go means letting the offender back into your life—or worse, excusing what they did.

But letting go is not about reconciliation. It is about **boundaries**. It is about choosing where you put your energy and attention. You can release the emotional grip of a past injustice without reopening the door to someone who caused harm.

Letting go might sound like:

- "I no longer think about you every day."
- "I don't relive the event anymore."
- "Your name no longer tightens my chest."
- "I still don't trust you, and I'm allowed to keep my distance."

This is **peace without permission**. You don't need the offender's apology to get there. You don't need society's approval to remain distant. You just need *yourself*—and the commitment to stop carrying what no longer helps you survive.

Rituals of Release

In many traditions, healing involves **ritual**—not religious necessarily, but symbolic acts that mark the shift from pain to peace. These rituals help externalize what we've held inside. They make the invisible visible. They create closure without the need for the other person's participation.

Examples include:

- Writing a letter to the person who hurt you—and burning it, burying it, or keeping it as a record.
- Creating a timeline of the experience to reclaim the narrative.
- Naming the lesson aloud: "This is what I know now."
- Holding a silent moment for the version of yourself that was hurt.
- Speaking your truth into a mirror or to a trusted confidant.

These small acts are powerful. They remind you that healing is not just mental—it is *embodied*. It lives in gesture, memory, space, and meaning.

Choosing Peace as a Form of Power

In previous chapters, we explored how grudges form from the loss of power—emotional, relational, moral. Peace, then, becomes a form of **reclaimed agency**. Not the denial of hurt, but the decision not to be held hostage by it.

Peace does not mean you no longer care.

It means you now **care about yourself more.**

It means:

- You've chosen growth over stagnation.
- You've released the fantasy of a better past.
- You've given yourself the love that others withheld.
- You've stopped waiting for closure that may never come.

Peace is not passive. It is one of the most **active, radical choices** you can make.

When Forgiveness Follows Peace (If It Ever Does)

For some, peace leads naturally to forgiveness. After the storm calms, after the clarity settles, they find space to say, "I forgive you"—not because they have to, but because they want to. Forgiveness, in this context, becomes a *gift*, not a transaction.

But for others, peace never leads to forgiveness—and that is **equally valid**. You may never forgive someone who violated you. You may never feel that reconciliation is appropriate. You may never be able to say "It's okay"—because it wasn't.

And yet, you may still smile. Still breathe deeply. Still love, trust, and live fully.

This is peace on your own terms.

In Summary

Peace is not the same as forgiveness. It does not require an apology, a reconciliation, or a clean emotional slate. It requires only that you **stop giving your power to a story that no longer defines you**.

You can live with pain without being ruled by it.

You can remember without being trapped.

You can speak your truth and still choose peace.

In the next chapter, we turn the lens outward—toward what happens when *you* are the one being resented. What does it mean to carry someone else's grudge? How do we handle being seen as the villain in someone else's story?

Chapter 11: When You're the One Being Resented

We spend much of this book examining what it means to hold a grudge. But what happens when you are the one **being resented**? When someone else holds on to a grievance about you—a moment, an action, a silence—that shaped their perception of who you are?

Few experiences are more uncomfortable than being cast in the role of the villain, especially when we don't agree with the narrative. Whether justified or misunderstood, being the object of someone else's resentment can provoke feelings of guilt, confusion, shame, and defensiveness.

This chapter is about what it means to live with the reality that someone may resent you. How do we respond to being seen as the cause of someone's pain? How do we handle the emotional complexity of *possibly* having done harm—and how do we move forward when there is no path to reconciliation?

Seeing Ourselves Through Their Eyes

Being resented often feels unjust, especially when we didn't intend harm. But the hardest truth in interpersonal conflict is this: **intent does not erase impact**. We may believe we were misunderstood. We may believe the other person is exaggerating, projecting, or refusing to let go. And we might be right.

But if we are serious about integrity, we must start with empathy.

Ask yourself:

- What might this person have experienced from their side?
- Is there truth in their perception—even if it wasn't my intention?
- Have I truly listened, or have I only defended myself?

Sometimes, people resent us not because we hurt them maliciously, but because we failed them emotionally. Because we disappeared when they needed us. Because we said nothing when they were drowning. Because we were too consumed with our own lives to recognize theirs unraveling.

This doesn't make us evil. It makes us human. But responsibility is not reserved only for villains. It also belongs to those willing to grow.

Defensive vs. Reflective Responses

When we learn that someone resents us, the natural instinct is to become **defensive**:

- "That's not what I meant."
- "They're being unfair."
- "I already apologized."
- "They're too sensitive."

These reactions are understandable. But they often close the door to understanding. A reflective response, by contrast, acknowledges the pain—even if we don't fully agree with the details.

A reflective posture sounds like:

- "I didn't realize how much that affected you."
- "I see now how I may have contributed to that."
- "Thank you for telling me, even if it's hard to hear."
- "I'm willing to revisit what happened with an open mind."

The goal is not to accept blame for everything. It's to stay present in the discomfort long enough to **learn something real**—about ourselves, about them, about the emotional weight of our interactions.

When You Did Do Harm

Sometimes, the resentment directed at you is not exaggerated. It's justified.

You hurt someone. You broke trust. You acted carelessly, selfishly, perhaps even cruelly. And now, they carry the emotional residue of that harm.

It's never easy to admit this. But acknowledgment is not the same as self-condemnation. Owning our mistakes is the foundation of **repair**—not just with others, but within ourselves.

If you've hurt someone and they still resent you:

- Accept that healing is on their timeline, not yours.
- Apologize sincerely, without qualifications or expectations.
- Avoid trying to "speed up" their forgiveness to relieve your guilt.

- Respect their boundaries—even if it means no longer being in their life.

True remorse is not about demanding reconciliation. It's about **restoring dignity**, even if only from afar.

When the Grudge Is Disproportionate or Misplaced

Not all resentment is fair. People may resent you for things outside your control. For saying no. For choosing yourself. For living a life they envy or don't understand. You may become the target of projected pain—someone else's wound seeking an outlet.

In such cases, the path forward involves:

- Recognizing the difference between **responsibility** and **projection**.
- Holding compassion without sacrificing your boundaries.
- Resisting the urge to "fix" a distorted narrative that isn't yours to rewrite.
- Accepting that you cannot control how others remember you.

Sometimes, all you can do is **stand in your truth** with humility—and let go of the need to be seen as right.

Living with an Unforgiven Version of Yourself

There may be people in your life—or in your past—who will never forgive you. No matter how much you grow, no matter how sincerely you apologize, they may continue to see you through the lens of who you once were.

This is one of the most difficult emotional truths to accept.

But it is also one of the most important: **you do not need to be forgiven to become better.**

You are not frozen in the version of yourself that hurt them. You are allowed to evolve—even if they never see it. Even if they never believe it. Your worth is not dependent on their absolution.

Forgive yourself—not to erase the past, but to make peace with it.

When Reconciliation Is Impossible

There are times when reconciliation is not possible or healthy. Perhaps the relationship was toxic. Perhaps trust cannot be rebuilt. Or perhaps too much time has passed, and the emotional distance is too great.

If reconciliation is not an option, focus instead on:

- Making peace with the fact that someone resents you.
- Honoring your growth, regardless of their forgiveness.
- Sending them silent goodwill, if that aligns with your values.
- Living in alignment with who you are now—not who you were then.

You can respect their pain without remaining trapped in it. You can carry your remorse without letting it drown you. And you can live forward—even if a part of your past remains unresolved.

In Summary

Being resented by someone else is deeply painful—especially when we don't fully agree with their version of events. But it also offers us a chance to examine who we were, who we are becoming, and what we want to take responsibility for.

Sometimes, we must accept that we are part of someone else's pain story—and we may never get the chance to rewrite it. But we can still write our own.

In the next chapter—the final chapter before the epilogue—we will explore what it means to hold on to a grudge **with intention**, or to let go with clarity—not because we are told to, but because we are ready.

Chapter 12: Letting Go—or Holding On With Intention

Letting go is often framed as the ultimate emotional victory—proof that we have healed, moved forward, and evolved. But letting go is not a moral obligation. It is a **personal decision**, and like any meaningful decision, it must come from a place of intention, not pressure.

At the same time, holding on to a grudge is not always a sign of bitterness or stagnation. It can be a deliberate choice—a way of preserving meaning, protecting boundaries, or honoring unresolved truth.

In this final chapter, we explore what it means to either let go or hold on **with awareness, with clarity**, and **without shame**. Because the true question is not *"Should I forgive?"*—but *"What is most honest for me now?"*

The Pressure to Move On

Culturally, we are inundated with messages that push us toward closure:

- "Let it go."
- "Don't dwell on the past."
- "You're only hurting yourself."

While these phrases may be well-intentioned, they often carry the implicit message that continuing to feel pain is a failure. But emotional pain is not weakness—it's evidence of depth, value, and impact. If something still hurts, it likely mattered.

When we are told to move on prematurely, we risk suppressing pain rather than processing it. We risk choosing **appearance over authenticity**.

Letting go must never be forced. It must be chosen. And it must be rooted in a sense of readiness—not moral pressure.

Letting Go as an Act of Clarity

When letting go is right, it often arrives not with fireworks, but with **quiet certainty**.

Letting go sounds like:

- "I don't need this story to define me anymore."
- "I've grieved this long enough."
- "They don't get to take any more of my energy."
- "I want to create space for something new."

It is not about forgetting or minimizing the offense. It's about **choosing emotional spaciousness** over emotional entanglement.

Letting go is not a declaration that what happened didn't matter. It's an acknowledgment that **you matter more**—your peace, your future, your emotional freedom.

The Empowerment of Holding On (When Intentional)

There are times when **holding on** is the most honest choice we can make. Not because we want to be angry forever, but because letting go too soon would require us to lie to ourselves.

We may hold on because:

- The harm remains unacknowledged.
- Justice was denied or distorted.
- The offender has not changed or apologized.
- The pain is still shaping who we are becoming.

In these cases, the grudge becomes a **reminder**, not a prison. It keeps us alert, discerning, and morally anchored.

This kind of holding on is **intentional**, not reactive. It does not consume or corrode us. It exists beside our other emotions—not in place of them.

Questions to Ask Yourself

Whether you are ready to release a grudge or still carrying one that protects you, consider asking:

- "Am I holding on to stay safe—or to stay angry?"
- "Is this grudge still serving me—or is it shaping me in ways I don't

want?"
- "What would I lose if I let this go? What might I gain?"
- "Do I feel more like myself with this grudge—or further away from who I want to be?"

These questions are not meant to push you toward any specific conclusion. They are meant to deepen your awareness. **You don't need to act—just understand.**

Choosing Meaning Over Morality

When it comes to resentment, many people wrestle with moral narratives: "Good people forgive." "Bad people hold grudges." But real life is more complicated. You are not morally deficient because you haven't forgiven. And you are not morally superior because you have.

What matters more than moral purity is **meaningful action**:

- Are you aware of what you're carrying?
- Are you acting from alignment, not avoidance?
- Are you open to growth, regardless of outcome?

Meaning is a far better guide than morality. It allows us to treat ourselves with honesty instead of judgment.

Permission to Choose

Ultimately, this chapter—and this book—is about giving you **permission.**

Permission to hold on, if that protects your truth.

Permission to let go, if that frees your spirit.

Permission to revisit the decision tomorrow, if today you're not ready.

Emotional healing is not a straight line. It's a spiral. We return to old hurts in new ways, see them from new angles, and make new choices—not because we failed before, but because we are constantly evolving.

In Summary

Letting go is not a destination—it's a decision. And holding on is not failure—it can be a form of **emotional wisdom**.

Whether you release the grudge or keep it close, what matters is that the choice is **yours**. Not inherited. Not forced. Not performative. But grounded, honest, and free.

In the epilogue that follows, we reflect on what grudges ultimately reveal—not just about pain, but about the profound need to be seen, heard, and understood as human.

Epilogue: What Grudges Teach Us About Being Human

Grudges are not flaws in the emotional system. They are evidence that something mattered—deeply, personally, morally. They are the soul's resistance to being ignored, erased, or minimized. They are the stories we refuse to forget, not because we enjoy the pain, but because the pain still speaks a truth that hasn't been heard.

Throughout this book, we've explored the many forms that resentment can take: quiet and seething, loud and righteous, slow-burning or sharply defined. We've seen how grudges can protect, poison, teach, or distort. We've learned that they are not inherently bad—but they are always trying to tell us something.

What, then, do grudges ultimately teach us about being human?

They teach us that we are **meaning-makers**—that we don't just feel pain, we **interpret** it. We attach it to our values, our dignity, our sense of right and wrong. A grudge is not just a memory; it's a moral statement.

They teach us that we long for **justice**, not just peace. That we are not always healed by forgetting—but sometimes by being heard. That truth, acknowledgment, and respect can matter just as much as apology and reconciliation.

They teach us about **emotional complexity**. That we can be hurt and still compassionate. That we can feel anger without being cruel. That we can forgive in one breath and ache again in the next. That contradictions are part of the human condition.

They teach us that we are shaped by our stories—and sometimes, by the chapters that have not yet been closed.

But most of all, grudges teach us that we are not as alone as we sometimes feel. That the things we carry in silence are more universal than we imagine. That somewhere, someone else is holding on to something they never told anyone. And that perhaps, just by naming it, we've made space for someone else to begin healing too.

If you've carried resentment, this book was for you. Not to tell you what to do with it—but to remind you that you're not wrong for having it.

You are not broken.

You are not bitter.
You are human.
And that is enough.

References

Note: The following works have informed or inspired the writing of this book. While not all were cited directly, they contributed valuable insight to its themes and perspective.

- Brown, Brené. *The Gifts of Imperfection*. Hazelden Publishing, 2010.
- Buddhist teachings on compassion and nonattachment
- Enright, Robert. *Forgiveness Is a Choice: A Step-by-Step Process for Resolving Anger and Restoring Hope*. American Psychological Association, 2001.
- Hooks, Bell. *All About Love: New Visions*. HarperCollins, 2000.
- Lerner, Harriet. *The Dance of Anger*. Harper Perennial, 1985.
- Nussbaum, Martha. *Anger and Forgiveness: Resentment, Generosity, Justice*. Oxford University Press, 2016.
- Panksepp, Jaak. *Affective Neuroscience: The Foundations of Human and Animal Emotions*. Oxford University Press, 1998.
- The Bible – New Testament teachings on forgiveness
- The Qur'an – selections from Surah Al-Baqarah and Surah Ash-Shura
- The Talmud – commentary on repentance and interpersonal harm
- Worthington, Everett. *Forgiveness and Reconciliation: Theory and Application*. Routledge, 2006.

About the Author

Dr. Hussam Atef Elkhatib is an author, researcher, and cultural critic whose work explores the intersections of psychology, morality, language, and identity. With a background in philosophical inquiry and human behavior, Dr. Elkhatib is committed to illuminating the emotional and ethical experiences that shape how we live, relate, and remember.

Known for blending academic insight with deeply human reflection, his writing speaks to readers who seek clarity not just in their thoughts—but in their hearts. His work is rooted in compassion, complexity, and the belief that emotional honesty is a path to healing—not weakness.

When not writing, Dr. Elkhatib continues his research into cultural narratives, emotional literacy, and the moral dimensions of modern life.

Books by the Author (Listed in chronological order of publication)

- *Moralities for Life: Thoughts and Behaviors Justified*
- *Who Are We: Seeing Ourselves through the Eyes of One Another*
- *Behind the Glare: Unpacking the Media's Sexualization of Women*
- *Shrouded in Words: A Comprehensive Journey through Euphemism*
- *Good versus Evil: What's Good and Evil*
- *Grudge: Understanding Resentment, Justice, and the Desire to Be Heard*

About This Book

Grudge: Understanding Resentment, Justice, and the Desire to Be Heard is a compassionate, in-depth exploration of why we hold on to emotional pain—and what it means when we can't or won't let go. Challenging the cultural narrative that sees resentment as weakness, this book reframes the grudge as a meaningful moral signal: a response to injustice, a protest against silence, and a yearning for dignity.

With clarity, warmth, and psychological insight, Dr. Hussam Atef Elkhatib guides readers through the layers of resentment—personal, relational, cultural, and spiritual—offering not quick fixes, but understanding. This book is not a manual on how to forgive. It is an invitation to listen to our pain with wisdom, courage, and grace.

www.ingramcontent.com/pod-product-compliance
Lightning Source LLC
LaVergne TN
LVHW090432210926
848480LV00002B/790

9798231628827